BESWICK PC

Val Baynton

SHIRE PUBLICATIONS

Published in Great Britain in 2012 by Shire Publications Ltd,
Midland House, West Way, Botley, Oxford OX2 0PH, UK.

44-02 23rd Street, Suite 219, Long Island City, NY 11101,
USA.

E-mail: shire@shirebooks.co.uk   www.shirebooks.co.uk

A CIP catalogue record for this book is available from the
British Library.

Shire Library no. 669.   ISBN-13: 978 0 74781 100 8

Val Baynton has asserted her right under the Copyright,
Designs and Patents Act, 1988, to be identified as the
author of this book.

Designed by Tony Truscott Designs, Sussex, UK
and typeset in Perpetua and Gill Sans.

Printed in China through Worldprint Ltd.

12 13 14 15 16   10 9 8 7 6 5 4 3 2 1

COVER IMAGE

Comical Rabbits 1967–73; Piglet, 1968–90, Psalm, Ann
Moore Up, 1975–82; Jersey Bull Ch. Dunsley Coy Boy,
1956–97; Foxhound, 1969–97; Lord Mayor water jug,
1961–7; Simpkin from the Beatrix Potter collection,
1975–83.

TITLE PAGE IMAGE

The 'Knight in Armour', sometimes called the 'Earl of
Warwick', by Arthur Gredington, produced from 1949 to
1973. This sculpture often featured as the frontispiece to
catalogues in the 1960s.

CONTENTS PAGE IMAGE

'Jess' and 'Kate' issued in a limited edition of one hundred,
201 Beswick England backstamp. The models were based
on two working sheepdogs owned by Roy Nelson, who
farms in the Yorkshire Dales.

DEDICATION

To Guy, Ellie and Rosie.

ACKNOWLEDGEMENTS

I am grateful to the following for help in the preparation of
this book: Morris Abbot, Bob and Irene Davidge, Phil
Guest, Guy Heath, Barry Hill, Beswick Ltd, Richard Holt,
The staff of Louis Taylor Fine Art Auctioneers and Valuers,
Hanley, Stoke-on-Trent, Harvey and Hazel May, Mike
Musk, Judith Stonestreet, Marilyn Sweet, Stoke-on-Trent
City Archives, Jane Varley.

I would like to thank the Beswick family, Beswick
employees and Beswick collectors and dealers for their
unhesitating enthusiasm in responding to my many
requests for information made since 1985, and Andrew
Eeley of The Image Factory, Stoke-on-Trent, for
photography.

The information about Nancy Catford (see page 20)
is courtesy of John Capper and the Grays Pottery resource
website (www.grayspottery.co.uk).

ILLUSTRATION ACKNOWLEDGEMENTS

Pottery Gazette and Glass Trade Review, now Tableware
International, pages 7, 12 (bottom), 13, 24, 38 (bottom),
39 (top); Beswick Ltd, pages 3, 6, 8, 9, 10, 14 (top), 15,
16, 18, 23, 26, 29 (top), 30, 34 (bottom), 36 (top), 38
(top), 39 (bottom), 40 (top), 42 (bottom), 43, 44 (top),
45 (bottom), 46, 48 (top), 49 to 62 (all); Marilyn Sweet,
page 28 (top).

Andrew Eeeley for remaining photography and product
loans as follows:

Morris Abbot, pages 1, 4, 12 (top right), 17, 19, 20, 21,
27, 29 (bottom), 31, 32, 33, 34 (top), 35, 36 (bottom),
37, 41, 42, 44 (bottom), 45 (top), 48 (bottom); Harvey
May, pages 12 (top left), 14 (bottom) and 22; Mike Musk
and Richard Holt, page 5.

Louis Taylor Fine Art Auctioneers & Valuers, Hanley Stoke-
on-Trent, cover image, pages 28 (bottom), 63, 40
(bottom); Authors Own Collection, page 14 (top).

CONTENTS

INTRODUCTION

Beswick's international reputation is based on its ceramic studies of animals, especially of horses and cattle, and of anthropomorphic models inspired by popular characters from literature, film and television. These ranges were introduced from the 1930s and evolved rapidly after the Second World War, but the company originated in the 1890s.

When the business was founded it was a small-scale pottery manufacturing a vast assortment of ornamental and useful wares for the home; the variety ranged from spittoons to mantelpiece figures and from bread trays to hand-painted vases. In the early years products were similar to those made by numerous local competitors, yet remarkably Beswick survived while many of these other firms have long since disappeared.

One of the reasons for the company's success was that the Beswick family, who ran the business until it was sold to Royal Doulton in 1969, understood that they had to make what the housewife or gift buyer wanted at a price that was affordable, and something for every taste and every pocket. So traditional styles were produced for as long as demand dictated, but new lines reflecting the trends and fashions of the day were regularly introduced as well.

Mantelpiece dogs were a constant part of Beswick production during the twentieth century. This pair dates from 1933 to 1955.

Quality was also important and formed an essential part of the appeal of both the animal sculptures, where meticulous modelling ensured anatomical accuracy, and of the small character studies, which faithfully reproduced the spirit and detail of original drawings by illustrators such as Beatrix Potter.

Beswick's products have found their way into the homes of animal and ceramic enthusiasts around the world. Well-made, yet affordable, the sculptures have graced the shelves of children's bedrooms and have been regularly handled by their young owners. The quirky humour and the decorative details of other designs have similarly attracted many collectors. Some of the early pieces, as well as some more recent models, have become comparatively rare and are eagerly sought at car boot sales, auctions and on eBay.

This book explores the development of Beswick, tracing its progress from what was essentially a very ordinary Victorian pottery to a twenty-first-century brand. It looks at its broad product mix and at some of the people involved, including the Beswick family, key sculptors and designers. It also places Beswick in the context of the twentieth-century ceramic industry with its continuing issues of mechanisation and contraction. The story is remarkable because Beswick has endured and because of the widespread popularity of its products; it has just as important a place in the overall history of the Potteries as larger companies, or of more prestigious firms or individuals who promoted avant-garde, but short-lived designs.

Selection of characters inspired by the illustrations of Beatrix Potter and introduced between 1948 and 2002. (Left to right) 'Old Mr Pricklepin' (1983–9), 'Duchess Holding a Pie' (1979–82), 'Peter Rabbit Gardening' (1998–9), 'Ginger' (1976–82), 'Head Gardener' (2002), 'Anna Maria' (1963–83), and 'Jemima Puddle-Duck' (1948–2002).

A FAMILY FIRM
1894–1925

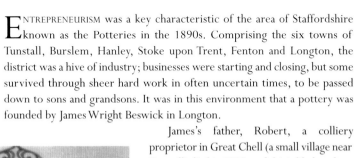

Entrepreneurism was a key characteristic of the area of Staffordshire known as the Potteries in the 1890s. Comprising the six towns of Tunstall, Burslem, Hanley, Stoke upon Trent, Fenton and Longton, the district was a hive of industry; businesses were starting and closing, but some survived through sheer hard work in often uncertain times, to be passed down to sons and grandsons. It was in this environment that a pottery was founded by James Wright Beswick in Longton.

James's father, Robert, a colliery proprietor in Great Chell (a small village near Tunstall) died in 1890, and this is likely to have provided the impetus and the finance to establish the pottery. There was family involvement in ceramic manufacture dating back to 1842, when Robert built and ran the Church Bank pottery in Tunstall. Later this was leased out to other potters on the understanding that they bought coal from the Beswick mine to fire the kilns. It is not recorded whether James and his elder brother, Robert, worked in the pottery but they were certainly involved in the colliery business, being listed as proprietors in the 1887 *Directory of the Potteries and District*. In 1890 they went their separate ways, Robert junior remaining at the colliery and in the family home, Chell House, and James moving to Longton, where, by 1896, his home is listed in local directories as Belgrave House, Dresden.

Involvement with Longton ceramic businesses dates from 1890, when Mrs J. W. Beswick became a partner of Thomas Heath at the Baltimore Works in Albion Street, as documented in the *PGGTR* in July 1913. Thomas Heath soon acquired another factory – the Albion Works in High Street – and both addresses were included in his advertisements until November that year, when mention of the Baltimore Works disappeared. In December 1893 the partnership was dissolved, allowing James Wright Beswick to open on his own account at the Baltimore Works in January 1894.

As his first advertisement, in the January 1894 issue of the *PGGTR*, records, J. W. Beswick specialised in 'Majolica and Earthenware', with wares including jugs, flower pots and pedestals, hanging pots, bread trays and cheese stands, as well as 'figures of all descriptions'. In July the *PGGTR* carried its first review of the firm, commenting on figures and dogs that were 'of the old-fashioned type; the latter seem to range from toy terriers to greyhounds; … in either pairs or in sets to match; in addition … there are the milkmaid and soldier sets.' The report praises the modelling and the variety of decoration such as enamelling, printing, gilding and hand-painting. Unfortunately these early wares are not marked with a backstamp, so the only way of identifying pieces is by comparison with descriptions (and illustrations from *c*. 1900) in the *PGGTR*.

From the outset the product range was extensive; it is likely that the firm bought moulds from another failing company or that the partnership with Heath enabled Beswick to use existing moulds. Heath had bought the moulds of Adams & Bromley in the summer of 1893 and by July 1894 the *PGGTR* notes that he was making good use of them, especially for the foreign market, so perhaps he no longer had use for some of his earlier shapes.

The Beswicks' foray into the pottery industry was successful. The business expanded – from the summer of 1896 producing bone china at the Britannia Works in High Street, and in 1898 occupying the Gold Street Works, which was to be the home of Beswick for the following hundred years. Rationalisation took place, with first the Baltimore Works closing, and by early 1905 the Britannia Works had been relinquished too. The Gold Street Works was described in the *PGGTR* in 1898 as 'a very modern and completely fitted up factory, thoroughly up to the times in every respect', but the Beswicks decided to supply bone china again and it was simpler to base

The first advertisement for J. W. Beswick appeared in the *Pottery Gazette and Glass Trade Review* (*PGGTR*) in 1894. This one dates from January 1895 and reveals a new range, 'Decorated Toilet'.

production at another factory since the body required a different clay recipe from that needed for earthenware, and different production conditions such as kiln temperature. Hence the firm of Bridgett & Bates was purchased in 1908; the business was carried on as before with Mr Bates staying on as manager. In 1915 china production moved to the Warwick China Works, also in Longton, where the trading name Beswick & Sons was used. Bone china products are often marked: the 'B & B' backstamp, either printed or impressed, as adopted by Bridgett & Bates, continued to be used, along with the appellation 'Aldwych China'. At the Warwick Works ware was marked 'B & S' and/or 'Warwick China'.

In many ways James Wright Beswick was a typical Victorian. He was married three times and had thirteen children, of whom only the eldest, John, and the youngest, Gilbert, born in 1904, are known to have worked in the family firm, and Gilbert's involvement was after James's own death in May 1920. The children were born over such an extended time, John being thirty-six when Gilbert was born, that Gilbert was seven years younger than his nephew, John Ewart, who was born in 1897. From 1934 to 1969 Gilbert and Ewart (representing the third generation of the family) ran the business together.

James believed in paternalistic values and established an ethos at the factory that was continued by his two sons and grandson. According to his obituary in the *PGGTR* in June 1920, 'it was a characteristic of him that he said what he meant and meant all he said, but he was invariably kind and generous withal.' All four Beswicks were regarded affectionately by their employees;

John Beswick
(1868–1934).

they were considered to be strict employers but at the same time were sensitive over welfare issues for their workforce. The decorating manager, Jim Hayward, later recalled that John Beswick gave every employee a card at Christmas containing a £1 bonus, reduced proportionately where appropriate to take account of workers who had not been employed for a full year.

John Beswick joined the business in the late 1890s, becoming a partner in 1905, on a salary of £4 per week, and with responsibility for production at the Gold Street Works. Unlike his father, who was a self-trained potter who had learned his skill solely through experience, John benefited from some technical training, attending the Tunstall Pottery School – but even so much of his knowledge was gained through practical experience.

John followed James's footsteps as a leader in the local community, as a justice of the peace and a

Stoke-on-Trent city councillor. Both were devout Methodists and the family was extensively involved with the Bourne Primitive Methodist Church in Longton – contributing towards a larger chapel in the early twentieth century.

Production up to around 1920 continued along the same lines as in the 1890s – with general earthenware, china and majolica goods, both useful and ornamental, being produced. Tableware patterns and shapes reflected fashions of the day and were decorated mainly by print and enamel techniques although some litho (lithographed) designs were used. Among the designs were embossed patterns, simple sprigs and festoons of flowers, strongly coloured Derbies (with Imari-styled decoration in the manner of Royal Crown Derby), and popular blue and white styles such as the Willow pattern. In 1911 the coronation of King George V was commemorated with a plate and a handled mug. Figures such as generals on horseback, gardeners and sportsmen, as well as mantelpiece ornaments portraying animals, remained in production, which were, as the *PGGTR* reported, 'much better finished than were formerly sold – and at no increase in price'. Another line was a mug with a frog at the bottom. Basic crockery was supplied to a variety of hospitals and institutions such as the London County Council Asylums Committee.

When James Wright Beswick died in 1920 John inherited the business, but it was not until January 1927 that the company name changed from J. W. Beswick to John Beswick. Perhaps there were some inheritance issues to be resolved.

Page from a catalogue of c. 1920 showing ewer and bowl sets and bone china cups. Each pattern was available as tea or breakfast sets.

TOILET SERVICES FOR ALL CLASSES.

"ALDWYCH" CHINA TEA SETS.

JOHN BESWICK, GOLD ST., LONGTON, STAFFS.

PEKIN No. 2
6660

CLYDE 6466

NANKIN No. 2
6662

CUBA No. 2 ON PED.
6661

DURBAR No. 1 ON PED.
6663

EGYPTIAN ON PED.
5057

BESWICK WARE 1925–40

T HE 1920s was a decade of change for the Beswick factory; most importantly, wares began to develop a distinctive look that enabled them to be differentiated from the output of other potteries.

One of John Beswick's first challenges was a 'sectional' strike at the Gold Street Works in March 1921. The dispute concerned pay rates for the biscuit and glost oven placers and how long the ovens (the kilns in which ware was fired) should take to fill. Other operatives downed tools 'in sympathy' and the factory was on strike for at least a week. A general miners' strike, which lasted three months, then complicated matters: when there was no coal, potteries could not fire their wares and so miners' strikes of more than a few days affected the whole industry and many potteries had to shut down. The exceptions were potteries that had their own source of coal or had reserve stocks. Miners' strikes were not new: this was the third in ten years and it made between thirty and forty thousand pottery operatives idle. Similar disruption affected the industry several times during the twentieth century, but most notably during the strikes of 1926. The need for a more reliable power source to fire the kilns was one of the factors behind the industry-wide development of alternative technology using gas later in the century.

By summer 1921 production resumed, and in the early autumn John Beswick made his debut as head of the company in the London market, where his wares were shown at the sample and show rooms of the firm's new pottery agent, Mr W. Bradbury. Extensive selections of inexpensive bone china teaware and 'earthenware table articles of all descriptions' were promoted. However, as the *PGGTR* reported, 'conspicuous amongst the more ambitiously decorated ornamental wares are some interesting lines in vases, floating bowls, rose-bowls, daffodil bowls, clock sets and trinket sets'.

In May 1925, the *PGGTR* noted that these ornamental wares were becoming increasingly important as production gradually shifted from cheap but useful earthenware with edge-line and sprig patterns to 'fancies'. One striking decoration popular throughout the 1920s was a design of pink roses

Opposite:
Elaborate vases
dating from the
early 1920s. Pekin,
Clyde, etc. are
shape names.

Matt glaze decoration: Trentham Art Ware nightlight holder (shape 354), continued in production with a Beswick backstamp after 1941; candle holder (shape 423), made in many different colours from 1936 to 1963.

interlinked with a trailing leaf in green and gold on a jet-black ground. Since ware from the Gold Street Works was not backstamped until after 1930, these pieces can be accurately identified only by their decoration number, 3072, or by an impressed shape name. Shape names were inspired by towns and cities, although there are some exceptions such as 'Eric' – possibly named after John's second son, who died in 1903. According to Jim Hayward, the plant-pot shape 'Douglas' was named after the Beswick family's holiday trips to the Isle of Man (Douglas being the island's capital). Other noteworthy designs from the period include the hand-painted and gilded 'Chinese Hut' on a choice of background colours – blue, helio (light to medium purple) or red (number 6116) – and a flying bluebird litho pattern (number 6155), which featured a selection of birds and butterflies against a vivid sky-blue and white ground. Numerous floral designs, and landscape scenes inspired by different countries such as Egypt, Italy and Holland, were also available. The Callows wrote in *The Charlton Standard Catalogue of Beswick Pottery* that decoration numbers had reached number 1000 by 1900, 2500 by 1914 and almost 7000 by 1932.

Advertisement from the *PGGTR*, 1930, showing the company name as John Beswick.

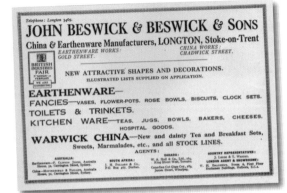

Investment in the Gold Street Works ensured more and better-quality products could be made, and the decorating manager, Mr Dean, was charged with creating innovative decorations. Two recruits in 1926 were Jim Hayward, who joined as a painter improver, and Albert Hallam, who was employed as an apprentice mould-maker; these were junior positions but the two men were to play essential roles in the future development of the company.

In 1927 a trade advertisement announced the new company name as John Beswick, as well as fresh decorations. These included designs combining lithos with relief modelling – used effectively on decoration number 6644, which featured a Dutch couple against a marine background, with an embossed pebble effect at the foot of the vases. A second development was matt glazes, sometimes combined with contemporary hand-painting to create artistic pieces influenced by the Art Deco styles of the time. Beswick was demonstrating his instinct – learnt from his father and passed down to his own son – of ensuring that Beswick products not only fulfilled the demands of the customers but were at a price that was affordable, especially in the 'somewhat economical times' observed by the *PGGTR* in September 1929, when people could not pay 'fancy' prices for their ornaments.

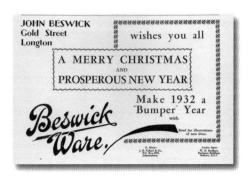

Advertisement from the *PGGTR* in December 1931, with the new Beswick Ware slogan introduced in 1930 adapted to wish retailers seasonal greetings.

Also important was the selection of shapes, and Beswick tempted customers by including in their ranges shapes that were both useful and ornamental – items such as cheese and butter dishes, biscuit barrels, and clocks; these fulfilled a useful function around the home but provided colour and novelty too. The Tudor Times Collection with its views of 'olde England' was popular, as was another design combining an all-over floral 'chintz' style pattern on a filigree background.

By late 1930 Beswick was firmly set on a new direction, as evidenced by the introduction of the bold Beswick Ware advertisement, the first time the name 'Beswick Ware' had been used, and the closure of the works in Chadwick Street, where Warwick China was made. Older-style decorations such as the black-grounded wares, imposing vases decorated in mazarine blue and gold, and even the Edwardian favourites of pot and pedestal and hanging pots remained available but were slowly being replaced by tableware sundries such as egg sets, cruets and 'cosy sets' (a teapot, hot-water jug and cream jug on a tray) in either traditional litho decorations or in ivory or blue matt glaze. Some of the novelty sets included animal forms such as the 'Duckling' egg set and the 'Chick' cruet, where the salt and pepper pots took the form of chickens (later given the number 1099 in the shape book).

The pottery worked hard at modelling new shapes, preparing the moulds and creating fresh decorations, and Salad and Gardena Ware and a series of jug-shaped flower holders were launched in late 1931 or early 1932. By this time Jim Hayward had been promoted to assistant decorating manager, and in this role his talent for shape design and decoration quickly became clear, as had Albert Hallam's skill at mould-making. Freelance modellers were still used for preparation of the shapes – and several names appear repeatedly in

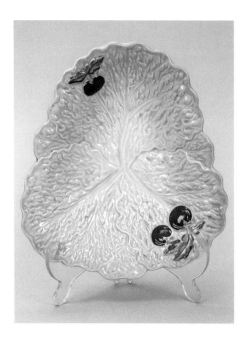

Salad Ware Tomato
Dish modelled by
Symcox, 1932–70.

the surviving factory records, such as Mr Symcox and Mr Owen; Symcox was paid £1 for each vase he modelled. The lettuce-leaf-shaped, embossed Salad Wares included salad bowls and servers, cucumber trays, tomato trays, celery trays, cheese and preserve pots, while the Gardena series, modelled in the form of flowers with embossments tinted in pastel shades, was more suitable for afternoon tea, with shapes such as sandwich sets, covered muffins, jugs, biscuit jars and a teapot. Jugs and vases were designed to compete with continental pottery and were gaily decorated in one of six different ultra-modern styles. Also popular in 1932 were lemon squeezers.

The 1920s and 1930s were a difficult period for trading, and every issue of the monthly *PGGTR* contains details of china dealers whose businesses had failed. Frequently the Beswick pottery was owed money by these shops, and in July 1932 Blackhurst & Hulme, the china-manufacturing business run by Wilfred Beswick, one of John's younger brothers, announced its insolvency. In the same issue other

Cup and saucer
in Cottage Ware
decoration made
from the late
1940s until
the 1960s.

Beswick Ware

COTTAGE SERIES

An attractive and unique range of splendidly modelled Cottage Ware, hand-painted in bright ceramic colourings, at attractive prices.

An ideal window display.

Catalogue page, pre-Second World War, showing Cottage Ware. Most of these shapes were made from 1933 until 1970.

companies to reveal ruinous financial problems included S. Winkle & Co, teapot manufacturers in Burslem, and H. T. Robinson of the Cauldon Potteries. Pottery manufacture was never easy and the number of factory closures since 1918, many due to economic conditions, was the subject of an article in September 1932. The author also noted the development of time-saving mechanical methods leading to the decline of hand production and the rise of short-time working, both resulting in less employment.

Over the next couple of years new modelled tableware series included Flowerkist, an embossed sweet-pea design on a wicker-effect ground, and Cottage Ware, with a choice of green or primrose ground. Both were shown at the British Industries Fair in 1933 and bought by Queen Mary and the Duchess of York. Also new was a range called Trentham Art Ware, which was designed and made by Beswick and sold exclusively by G. Hardy & Co, a Nottingham-based general ceramic wholesaler.

This relationship with Hardy's was an essential part of Beswick's success in the 1930s. The wholesaler imported various ornamental and sculptural products from the Continent, especially art wares from Spain, Italy and Holland, but the company was more than happy to buy from Beswick if the pottery could make a similar style at a good price. Matt-glazed wares, a series of ornately carved vases and jugs called Modelle Ware, figures, dogs and all kinds of animals became part of the Trentham Art Ware range. An example of a piece that Beswick may have been asked to imitate in 1936 is a wall mask of

Page from Jim Hayward's shape book, showing the 'Tyrolean Lady' wall mask commissioned by Hardy's, and a range of other shapes by the modellers of the decade – Miss Greaves and Mr Symcox. Designs are categorised with 'B' for Beswick and 'H' for Hardy's, and costings are included for some items. A large cross indicates the piece was subsequently withdrawn. Shape 454 is illustrated on page 20.

The humorous 'Penguin Family' modelled by Arthur Gredington has charmed many collectors. They were issued between 1940 and 1973.

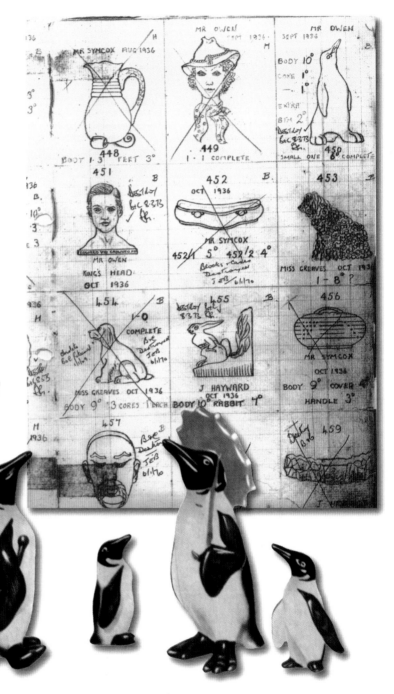

a woman in a Tyrolean-style hat, shape number 449, that is almost identical to Goldscheider model number 7176, dating from 1935 or earlier (illustrated in Ora Pinhas's authoritative study of the Austrian company, page 169). In the factory shape book, pieces reserved for Hardy's were marked with an 'H' and those issued with a Beswick backstamp with a 'B'.

'Panda with Ball' and 'Panda Cub' in blue glaze, 1934–54.

When the agreement with Hardy's ended in 1941 many of the pieces that had been made exclusively for them, such as the set of comical penguins (shapes 800–3), were made with a Beswick backstamp, but if there was a very similar piece already in the Beswick range, then it is highly likely that production of the Hardy's shape ended.

1934 was a significant year for the Beswick pottery. Shape development continued apace – over one hundred new shapes had been modelled in the previous twelve months – and Jim Hayward had replaced Mr Dean as decorating manager. Hayward was educated at the local art school in Stoke-on-Trent, where one of his tutors was the eminent ceramic designer Gordon Forsyth, and at the Technical College in Burslem and he applied the latest theories about design and management to Beswick production. He introduced a shape book, systematically listing every new shape that was modelled and approved for mould-making. He entered existing shapes into this book – giving numbers to vases and jugs that were previously identified by a name – and then meticulously recorded new shapes as they were developed. The retrospective recording of shapes is not necessarily in the order they were originally created – since a dog bookend first referred to in contemporary press reports in 1934 is shape 87, and the Salad Wares that were available by 1932 have numbers from 210 onwards. The earliest date recorded is 1935, against shape 370, and from then on month and year are noted consistently. Another improvement Hayward instituted was to change the colour tone used on Salad Wares, introducing a paler green and shading to give a more delicate effect around the leaves.

Jim Hayward's work with matt glazes was recognised by John Beswick, especially his talent for using the quality and colour of glaze and its texture for making patterns. Extensions and structural developments at the factory provided proper mixing facilities for the glazes; when Hayward started experimenting with glazes he did it outside, measuring quantities by slop weight and by eye, and combining all the ingredients by hand. The extensions included accommodation for the growing number of matt-glaze workers, for at the height of the technique's popularity there were around fifty such

Ewart and Gilbert
Beswick.

female decorators. Some pieces, such as 'Wonderland', a pattern of rabbits in woodland, and 'Aloma', a design of cactus trees, were decorated over the glaze, either with a hand-painted enamel decoration or by tube lining. Colours included lilac and 'Bark', the apt name for the chocolate-brown effect, and the glazes were applied not just to vases, jugs and plant pots but to animals and other novelty shapes. Many of the shapes in the 1930s and 1940s were originated by Jim Hayward, although other people were commissioned to model them to his design. He was thus one of the few ceramicists of the era responsible for both shape and decorative design.

On 16 October 1934 John Beswick died. For the few years before his death he had been much involved with local politics and other community affairs, and so his son, John Ewart (known by his second name), had gradually assumed more responsibility and was probably behind the upbeat marketing and modern product that typified the Beswick ranges from 1930 onwards. John was greatly respected, and his funeral, described in the *Evening Sentinel,* was attended by representatives of the City Council, churches and public bodies, as well as from within the industry. Among around a hundred floral wreaths were separate

Page from a catalogue dating from the mid- to late 1930s, showing a range of vases and jugs with matt glaze decoration, and an ashtray with a modelled Scottie dog. 'Moderne', 'Hyacinth', 'Rydal', etc, are pattern names, and the codes 88 to 180 are shape numbers.

tributes from several departments at the Gold Street Works – from the staff, warehouse and office, casters and clay workers, biscuit warehouse, biscuit aerographers, matt-glaze department, sliphouse and engineers, decorators and glost aerographers. Albert Hallam was a pall-bearer, along with two other Gold Street staff.

Ewart (named after William Ewart Gladstone, a staunch liberal and Methodist much admired by both John and James Wright Beswick) was born in 1897. His only brother, Eric, had died aged four in 1903, and he had two sisters, Dorothy and Gladys. After serving in the First World War, he returned to Stoke, where he played football for Stoke City. In February 1938 the *PGGTR* announced that Ewart had become Chairman and Managing Director, and Dorothy and Gladys became directors of the re-formed company, John Beswick Limited, jointly investing £20,000 in

shares of £1 each. Dorothy and Gladys were both regular visitors and workers at the pottery, especially during the Second World War. Also involved was Gilbert, Ewart's uncle, who was appointed sales director in 1957, when the company became publicly limited.

Ranges launched in the thirties included novelties such as a pair of bookends with a begging dog, a mirror stand with a polar bear, animal and

Indian wall mask modelled by Mr Dean, 1934–54. In the 1930s the wholesale price was 21s a dozen.

'Galleon' plaque modelled by Mr Fletcher and available in various matt glaze colourings. This is decoration number 7714, made from 1934 to 1954. 'Sealyham' wall plaque (shape 373), modelled by Mr Watkin: one of three plaques with and without bows made between c. 1934 and c. 1940 and originally exclusive to Hardy's.

'Seated Puppy Dog', modelled by Miss Greaves, and obsolete by 1969.

These dogs modelled by Mr Watkin are among the earliest of the freestanding animals launched in the 1930s. Different decorative treatments including blue gloss, white gloss and white and tan were available. The dogs were discontinued by 1967.

figurative sculptures and wall masks portraying a variety of characters such as Tony Weller (inspired by Charles Dickens's *Pickwick Papers*), an Indian Brave, jesters and contemporary-style young women. To keep up with all these new designs, more freelance modellers were employed – including Messrs Watkin, White and Fletcher and Misses Greaves and Catford. Anna Edith Catford, known as Nancy, had studied at the School of Woodcarving in South Kensington but moved to the Potteries in the mid-1930s as she wanted to develop her ceramic modelling skills. She worked as a freelance modeller for the ceramic industry, specialising in birds and animals – and for Beswick she did several pieces, including a set of toothbrush holders featuring a hiking dog, keep-fit elephant, gamekeeper fox and golfer rabbit.

Miss Greaves's collection of humorous stylised animals, including frolicking lambs, daft ducks, cute rabbits, frogs, dogs and a bashful squirrel,

Left and below: Animals by Miss Greaves advertised as 'Distinctive Pottery at moderate prices featuring the modern trend in matt glaze effects' (*PGGTR*, April 1936). Duck and squirrel in cream satin matt glaze, c. 1936–54.

decorated in a cream matt glaze and a soft blue gloss were popular – and she also created a collection of small child studies that are hard to find today. Mr Watkin's work is among the most recognisable of Beswick wares – including flying-bird wall plaques and a cruet depicting the comedians Laurel and Hardy.

Eric Owen, a good friend of Jim Hayward, modelled naturalistic designs and character ware at home in the evenings, since by day he was employed by the prestigious Minton company. He modelled a bust of Edward VIII for

Two more models by Miss Greaves showing blue gloss glaze. Lamb and Donkey, c. 1936–54.

555555544

'Duck' nightlight holder modelled by Mr Watkin and produced from 1939 to 1954.

'Butcher Boy' and 'Gypsy Girl': two of a variety of figural subjects modelled between 1936 and 1969; these two date from 1947 to 1958 and were the work of Arthur Gredington.

the coronation in 1937 but the majority of designs for this occasion were by Felix Weiss. All were hastily adapted following Edward's abdication before he was crowned. Owen recommended other modellers, including Arthur Gredington, to Hayward.

Gredington had worked for Wedgwood before winning a scholarship to study at the Royal College of Art for three years. When he returned to Stoke, he became Beswick's first resident modeller in 1939. He set to work modelling designs already in the pipeline,

Catalogue page showing a selection of animals and birds modelled by Watkin and Gredington in 1939. The horse Bois Roussel was the inspiration for shape 701 (centre bottom row). Horse number 766 is unusual for the period since it is modelled on a base, and, despite its appearance in this catalogue, an example has not been found. It is possible it was originally made for Hardy's and was never put into production with a Beswick backstamp.

but in March two realistic sculptures – of a deer on a rocky mound and a racehorse – revealed that a new era was underway, that of accurate models of specific animal champions and named breeds.

Catalogue page showing flying-bird wall plaques including seagulls, mallards, pheasants, blue tits, kingfishers and swallows. Other bird species made were flamingo, humming bird, pink-legged partridge, green woodpecker and teal.

1886/9674
4"

1885/9674
4½"

1880/9675
5½"

1867/9675
8½"

1877/9675
6½"

1898/9662
5"

1883/9662
6½"

1876/9
3½"

Cats for Collectors BESWICK Beautiful new Mod
STOKE-ON-TRENT ENGLAND

COMPLETE RANGE IN
WHITE 9662
BROWN TABBY 9674
BLUE 9675 AND SIAMESE

1897
6½"

1882
9½"

1887
4½"

ANIMALS COME OF AGE
1940-69

PROSPECTS SEEMED GOOD at the beginning of 1939: the factory expansion and redevelopment programme, creating a more efficient production flow, was almost finished; a good creative team of designer, modeller and mould-maker was in place; products were selling well; but then war was declared.

The industry generally, and Beswick specifically, saw that the war provided opportunities to gain overseas markets – by manufacturing ceramics that were previously made in Germany, Italy or Czechoslovakia. Two new sgraffito series, Venetian and Florentine, were rapidly designed and launched. Florentine, with a bird, was initially sold through Hardy's, and Venetian, with flowers, had a Beswick backstamp. Both designs were available in several colours, including green, blue and red, as well as plain white. The Kindergarten series of twelve figurines followed; this was based on the sentimental child studies created by Sister Hummel and made by the German maker Goebel before the war (and again afterwards).

As well as these new lines, and patriotic designs such as character mugs depicting a sailor, soldier and airman, a figure and a Toby jug depicting Winston Churchill, many other wares were available for export. These included flying-bird wall plaques, horses, useful ornamental jugs, vases and other shapes, motto wares, and boxed novelties such as sweet dishes, knives and spoons. Indeed, by 1942, (the *PGGTR* noted) 80 per cent of output was exported to Australia, South Africa, Canada, South America and New Zealand.

For the domestic market, however, strict rules and rationing were enforced. In 1942 Beswick was licensed to make undecorated earthenware and these utility wares were marked with a letter A. All manufacturers permitted to continue making pottery (and many were not) were categorised as Group I, II or III, depending on the maximum price each charged for its wares. Group III makers included Beswick and industry stalwarts such as Moorcroft, Royal Doulton and Josiah Wedgwood. Beswick also supplied the Royal Air Force with teapots, jugs, cups, saucers and jam dishes. The list was amended in 1945.

Opposite:
The front cover of the May 1964 *PGGTR* revealed the beauty of Hallam's cat collection and gave these descriptions: a long-haired 'Chinchilla' (more often called 'Persian') with emerald-green eyes; 'Long Haired Brown Tabbies' with typical, dense black markings; 'Blue Persians' with copper-coloured eyes; 'Short Haired White' with sapphire-blue eyes; 'Brown Tabby'; 'British Blue'; and 'Seal Point Siamese'.

Christmas in the decorating department. It was a factory tradition to hang decorations to celebrate the season.

View of the Gold Street Works in 1939. The front is typical of many nineteenth-century factory façades, with a central archway. To the right is the new three-storey extension, the culmination of development work made throughout the 1930s to modernise and expand production.

Members of the Beswick family and many factory employees served in the armed forces during the war. The *PGGTR* regularly announced awards made for bravery and enterprise and in January 1944 it noted that Lieutenant Peter Wild, grandson of James Wright Beswick and nephew of Ewart, had been awarded the Distinguished Service Cross.

The war years were prolific in terms of design, with nearly 280 shapes being added between September 1939 and June 1945, and the majority of these were modelled by Arthur Gredington. In March 1939 he unveiled a sculpture based on Bois Roussel, the surprise winner of the 1938 Epsom Derby. This was the horse's second race and he was to run only once more before being retired to stud, where he sired several champions over the following decade or so. As a ceramic model, however, Bois Roussel is even more famous, as this was the first of many Beswick sculptures based on racehorses, and a version remained in production until 2002.

In early models (up to *c.* 1947) the whole length of the tail was attached to the hind legs but in later versions only the end of the tail touches the leg. Like many Beswick horses, it was decorated in a variety of colours, from chestnut to 'Rocking Horse Grey' and from light to dark brown, in both gloss and matt glaze. This assortment of finishes rather detracts from the authenticity of the original sculpture, and later

'Huntsman' and 'Huntswoman', both modelled by Gredington and produced in a range of colours such as grey, brown and white; foxhounds 944 and 942 (first version); and fox.

'Large Hunter',
first version,
shape 1734.

Three horses
modelled by
Gredington: 'Pinto
Pony in Skewbald',
(1955, but at some
point modified so
that the tail hung
away from the
leg – note the
promotional
sticker);
Appaloosa Stallion
1967–89 and
1999–2002; Girl
on Pony 1957–65.

Selection of
backstamps in use
in the late 1960s.

racehorses, such as Arkle and Red Rum, were decorated in only one colour, to match the actual horse.

Bois Roussel was followed by other horses, including foals in playful poses, Shires and hunters. It is possible that ideas for a few of the early models, including a huntswoman jumping a fence and a rearing horse on a base, came from the German company Hertwig, which was making very similar models before the war, but soon Gredington was modelling original designs and, as collector Malcolm Middleton noted in *Collecting Doulton and Beswick* magazine issue 100, by the 1950s the Beswick brand was firmly associated with horse sculptures.

Horse models were successful because Beswick consistently invested in modelling, ensuring that the basic anatomy and conformity of the model were correct. Equally important was the flair of the individual sculptor in capturing

'The Queen on Imperial' and 'The Duke of Edinburgh on Alamein', modelled by Ted Folkard and issued between 1958 and 1981. 'Imperial' was also issued as a freestanding model in a variety of colourways until 1982.

the spirit of the horse in the finished piece; this was particularly important when modelling a champion or named breed. Gredington had this talent and so did Graham Tongue, who followed in his footsteps later in the century.

Outstanding among the horses is the series based on mountain and moorland ponies, developed from an idea by the equine expert Reginald Sherriff Summerhays. Familiar with Beswick's realistic models such as the hackney 'Black Magic of Nork', he thought there would be demand for more authentic studies. He perceived that horse lovers wanted art forms portraying horses to be as accurate as possible, but that bronze sculptures, for example, were frequently too expensive. Ceramic models were more affordable and so he wrote to Beswick suggesting that more should be made. He quickly received a reply asking him to suggest some breeds and oversee them through their design stages.

He later wrote an article entitled 'Horses and Ponies in Pottery', which appeared in the annual publication *The Horseman's Year*: 'This was something I could never have visualised, but which proved to be quite the most fascinating work I have ever been associated with in my long life with horses.' Nine breeds – New Forest, Dartmoor, Exmoor, Welsh Mountain, Fell, Dales, Highland, Shetland and Connemara – were produced, and Summerhays approved them at every stage. He praised the work of Hayward and Gredington and described his pleasure in seeing the transformation of the New Forest stallion:

The Fell pony and New Forest pony from a special catalogue promoting the Mountain and Moorland Pony range, with text by Summerhays, c. 1969.

When the damp clay model was put before me ... its head was most noticeably that of a horse. I mention this because it was an early instance of the skill of the modeller, when with a little off here, a certain shaping there, one or two other touches, the horse's head was changed magically to that of a pony.

Other horses created with his input include a Welsh Cob and a Thoroughbred mare with foal. Summerhays also notes the importance of the ceramic models as references illustrating the accepted standards for each breed in the mid-twentieth century.

From the 1940s animal modelling evolved rapidly and a veritable zoo of cattle, pigs, sheep, birds, dogs, fish, butterflies, elephants, zebras, pandas, bears and giraffes was introduced. Some were humorous studies

NEW FOREST PONY
Champion Stallion 'Jonathen 3rd'
1646 7in 18cm

NEW FOREST
This is a family pony if ever there was one, for example, the Forester will carry not only the children but the parents as well. In height it runs from quite a small pony up to 14-2 hands, which is the limit to the size of any pony. It is a real riding type, and has the advantage of being probably the most docile and tractable of any, and, added to this, there are possibly more of this breed to be found than any other. There is a nice choice of colour to be had, for none is barred and nowadays they are bred to such a correct type that you may well find yourself with a show pony. And if we wish to add to these good points, the New Forest makes a very useful polo pony and is pretty good in harness too.

FELL
This pony too is of the strong and sturdy type, a great and nimble hill climber and a most likeable fellow. Its average height is 13·3 hands and it carries some hair, or feather as it is called, on the heels. Less of a riding type perhaps, the Fell is very strong and, for centuries, was used as a pack animal, to carry lead from the mines to the nearby ports of shipment. None the less the Fell is claimed to be an excellent ride, as well as drive pony and this is justified. Although all colours are found, the typical colour is undoubtedly jet black. The Fell makes a very distinctive and attractive exhibit in the show ring and in recent years has swept into popularity in the south of England. A noticeable feature of the pony is its long curly hair. The fells of Westmorland and Cumberland are its original and natural home.

FELL PONY
Champion Mare
"Dene Dauntless"
1647 6½in 17cm

'Oceanic Bonito Fish' by Gredington, 1952–68, and 'Purple Emperor Butterfly' by Hallam, 1957–63. Such was the desire for authenticity that every scale was counted in fish models such as this.

A cheerful 'Cockerel' and 'Rooster' by Gredington, issued from 1944 to 1959.

This striking model by Gredington was made from 1960 to 1975 and shows an elephant being attacked by a tiger, revealing that Beswick was not afraid to depict the savagery of nature as well as its more benign side.

Wild animals including zebra, elephant, bear and giraffe, all modelled by Gredington in the 1940s and 1950s.

Garden birds have always been a favourite with Beswick collectors and versions have been in production since the 1940s: 'Great Tit' by Martyn Alcock, 1990–5; 'Whitethroat' (with mouth open) by Graham Tongue, 1967–73; and the first versions of 'Wren' and 'Chaffinch', both on a green mound, by Arthur Gredington, 1943–73.

emphasising the pathos or sentimental character of a breed, but increasingly animal sculpture was as realistic as possible and studies were based on real examples. Eight dog breed champions were added in 1941, including the Dalmatian Arnoldene and the Irish Setter Sugar of Wendover; this was the start of an extensive range covering most of the popular breeds of dog.

Close observation of live animals was sometimes a challenge for the modellers: Gredington was said to be terrified of cows and he would observe them only if he was safely behind a secure fence. In the 1950s the sculptor Colin Melbourne went to Chester Zoo to study lions; he was allowed to work from a raised platform inside the animals' enclosure but was petrified when one of the lions suddenly roared and tried to jump on to his perch.

Marketing initiatives were important. In December 1962 Beswick produced a small (2¼-inch) model of a giant panda (shape 1815) to support the British National Appeal of the World Wildlife Fund. For every model sold, Beswick made a donation to the fund. In 1964, to provide Australian interest on the stand at the Sydney Exhibition, a Merino ram

'Barn Owl' modelled by Gredington – the first version with split tail feathers.

They look docile, but to Gredington cattle were a source of terror: the Hereford family calf, bull and cow.

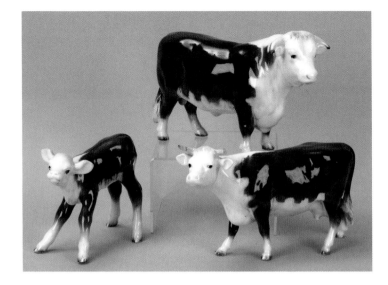

A herd of cattle from a catalogue dating from the late 1960s.

1740—5¼"
HIGHLAND COW

1827—3"
HIGHLAND CALF

2008—5"
HIGHLAND BULL

1350—5"
AYRSHIRE COW CHAMPION
ICKHAM BESSIE

1504—5"
CHAMPION
DAIRY SHORTHORN BULL
GWERSYLT LORD OXFORD 74th

1406/9333—3"
SHORTHORN

1510—4¼"
CHAMPION
DAIRY SHORTHORN COW
EATON WILD EYES 91st

1249/9200—2¼"
AYRSHIRE

1360—4¼"
HEREFORD COW
Polled Herefords can be supplied

1406/9202—3"
HEREFORD

1363—4¼"
HEREFORD BULL

1454—5¼"
CHAMPION
WHITEHILL MANDATE
AYRSHIRE BULL

22

(shape 1917) was modelled. This was based on the ram that was Grand Champion at the 1960 Sydney Show. Examples were sold with a special 'swing' label recording this detail, but it is unlikely that many of these will have survived. The model is rare as it was not produced after 1967.

Often it was necessary to take elements from several animals to get the ideal shape, especially when modelling dogs or cattle, as owners and breed experts often hold contrary opinions about what constitutes the perfect specimen. For the Fireside Collection, the Dalmatian was a combination of two bitches; both were owned by Gilbert Beswick's next-door neighbour, who happened to be a Dalmatian breeder.

By the 1960s Arthur Gredington was experiencing health problems and rarely came into the studio, preferring to work at home. He eventually retired in 1968, having made an exceptional contribution to animal sculpture. Albert Hallam progressively turned to modelling in his place and in 1964 a feline collection, created with the help and guidance

Above: 'Galloway Bull-Belted' by Gredington is one of the most desirable of Beswick models, 1963–9.

Above: The 'Merino Ram' made primarily for the Australian market, 1964–7, is sought after by collectors.

Left: Three pandas: 'Chi Chi', made for the British Museum from 1978 to 1980; 'Panda' by Watkin, 1939–54; and the cub made to support the World Wildlife Fund and issued from 1962.

of an expert cat breeder, was launched. Hallam also modelled tableware, birds and horses.

In 1967 the most prestigious of the realistically modelled sculptures, including horses, wild animals, birds, cattle and dogs, were marketed as the Connoisseur Collection. Among new models was Arkle – the first in a series of famous horses that later included Cardigan Bay, Nijinsky, Red Rum, Psalm and Grundy, modelled both with and without a jockey.

Opposite top: The Fireside Collection was launched at the end of the 1960s and most of the oversized models remained in production until 1989. ('Dalmatian' is about 32 cm high)

Left: 'Red Rum with Brian Fletcher Up', Connoisseur Collection; modelled by Tongue, 1975–82.

Graham Tongue, a passionate animal lover, joined the pottery in 1966. Initially modelling tableware, he soon graduated to animal sculpture, and many of the later additions to the Connoisseur Collection were his work.

The first literary characters to be produced by Beswick were inspired by the scenes described in *Alice's Adventures in Wonderland* and date from around 1940. A freelance modeller, Miss Joachim, created the series of wall plaques, but they were of limited success and are unlikely to have been made for long. Far more successful was the series of small-scale figurines based on the illustrations by Beatrix Potter. Ewart's wife, Lucy, is credited with the initial idea, conceived while on a family holiday in the Lake District in 1947. Jim Hayward acted promptly on the suggestion, and soon Arthur Gredington's models began to appear. Copyright clearances and design approvals had to be gained from Frederick Warne, the publisher of Beatrix Potter's *Tales*, but once these were in place the collection was unveiled with much success.

Among the first twelve studies were Jemima Puddle-Duck and Peter Rabbit, but more than one hundred distinct models were to follow at regular

Opposite bottom: A collection of cats, including the 'Cat Orchestra' by Gredington; one of a pair of large cats, also made in white with zodiac symbols, modelled by Pal Zalmen; 'Cat', looking up, modelled by Colin Melbourne; and 'Cat' scratching its ear, in the unusual British Blue colourway by Hallam.

Catalogue page dating from the late 1950s showing a selection of Beatrix Potter figures, Including the rare 'Duchess with Flowers', (bottom left) made between 1955 and 1967.

1966 was the centenary of the birth of Beatrix Potter and Beswick designed this advertisement in celebration (*PGGTR*, 1966).

intervals over the next fifty-five years. Several are available in different versions after the model was adjusted because of production issues with the original piece. This makes some models very much more sought-after than others. There are also many backstamp variations, which some collectors like to consider when forming collections.

The success of the Beatrix Potter range gave the Beswicks the confidence to add other characters from film and literature, and subjects from David Hand's *Animaland*, and from Walt Disney, including Mickey and Minnie Mouse, Snow White, Peter Pan and Winnie the Pooh, provided plentiful inspiration over the next couple of decades. Beswick was the first company in the United Kingdom to be given the right to produce Winnie the Pooh figurines, the launch of the collection coinciding with the Disney featurette, 'Winnie the Pooh and the Blustery Day', showing how highly Beswick's reputation for this type of licensed character ware was regarded.

Complementing the anthropomorphic collections were two series of naively modelled figurines, one portraying European nationals in traditional costumes carrying out farming activities, and the other a range of ethnic dancers. Many of these were by Jan Granowska, an emigrant from eastern Europe, and reflect her cultural roots.

In the late 1950s Ewart Beswick met Colin Melbourne, a sculptor and graduate of the Royal College of Art. As a result Ewart gave Melbourne the opportunity to design and model a contemporary collection that would compete with the low-quality 'moderne' ornaments being imported from the Continent. A small studio with a special decorating and glazing area was set up and the CM series was displayed in a separate showroom at Gold Street. Melbourne's stylised cats, bison, birds and other animals, as well as vases, were decorated with abstract motifs and unusual colours such as red, grey and yellow. The series was praised by the March issue of *Design*, the magazine of the Design Council, in 1957 for its quality and standard of design.

But the collection did not sell well and it was retired by the end of the 1960s. One of the reasons for Beswick's success was that less popular items were ruthlessly discontinued; otherwise, low-

Winnie the Pooh characters joined the Beswick collection in 1969. (*PGGTR*, 1969)

Disney's Snow White and the Seven Dwarfs and a pair of Jan Granowska's figurines, as shown in a catalogue of around 1958.

The CM series from a catalogue dating from c. 1958. A range of shapes and decorations is shown. Ornamental vases and bowls also designed by Colin Melbourne featured in the series too.

CONTEMPORARY FIGURES

Bedtime Chorus collection modelled by Hallam 1962–69. A cat and a dog singing were also designed to be part of this series.

volume pieces would have disrupted and reduced overall production output. For factories to survive, then as now, production had to be at the right rate, at the right price, and continuous for efficiency. Beswick wares were never intended to be highly collectable or unique, but they were intended to be

well made, well designed and affordable to all, and only by ensuring cost-effective production could this be achieved.

There was an ongoing debate in the industry, monitored in the *PGGTR*, about how to match demand to production. In spring 1961 a conference of retailers and manufacturers revealed diverging opinions – retailers thought potters should send staff to spend time in-store so they could understand the demands of customers, but potters thought design students and buyers should spend time on the factory floor to appreciate the difficulties of production.

The Beswicks shared in other industry debates such as about the importance of design and the need to export, but they had pragmatic views. For example, Gilbert Beswick was aware that overseas markets did not always want the same designs as the British customer, and therefore businesses could not always quickly meet government demands 'to increase exports'.

The era 1940 to 1970 may well be characterised by the coming of animals to Beswick but ornaments such as flower vases and jugs, series of useful and decorative wares and more standard tablewares continued to be important. As this range of wares suggests, the well-established Beswick policy of 'something for every taste and pocket' still held firm.

Series designed before the Second World War were generally not made much after 1950, although popular shapes in the Salad and Cottage series continued in production until *c.* 1970. New series such as the exotic 'Palm Tree' and the elaborate coral and seashell decorated plant and flower pots were made alongside contemporary *hors d'oeuvres* sets and more traditional embossed patterns such as 'Springtime', 'Tit Willow', 'Strawberry Fair' and

Elaborately relief-decorated coral and shell vases, modelled by Hallam and part of a larger range of similarly decorated pieces, 1965–72.

Plant holder designed by Kathi Urbach and issued in various colours between 1959 and 1965.

the literature-inspired Shakespeare series. Occasionally designs submitted by freelance ceramic designers were modelled – such as a small range of pieces by Kathi Urbach made in the late 1950s.

Various traditional and contemporary lithographed designs were issued in four tableware shapes – 'Contemporary', 'Eton', 'Marie' and 'Orbit'. Some patterns can be found on all ranges, but others are more specific. In the 1950s patterns such as 'Circus' and 'Ballet' revealed a modern approach to design, a trend that continued in the 1960s with 'Apollo', 'Lunar', 'Metric' and 'Verona' patterns, which were advertised as the 'Trendsetters' range. These were designed by Harry Sales, who joined the Beswick team in 1961. 'Zorba' tableware, introduced in 1969, with incised geometric shapes and produced in bronze or olive green, included the latest oven to tableware shapes, such as casserole dishes and roasters, and was promoted rather romantically as serving 'sunlight with every meal'. Nurseryware was also produced in patterns such as 'Disneyland', 'Nursery Rhymes' and 'Jack and Jill'.

Flower vases and plant pots were decorated in countless ways, some with simple painted designs, copper lustre, pewter effects or matt glazes. Others featured modelled relief decoration, ranging from a serene scene of deer grazing (shape 1051) to elaborate fern and floral forms (shapes 1191, 1295 and 1605). New effects were constantly being developed – the ongoing work of the art director, Jim Hayward, whose understanding of the chemistry of glazes and colour, combined with a fine graphic skill, resulted in distinctive effects that were frequently seen at their best on ornamental wares. He designed almost three thousand different decorations and also trained the senior paintresses in the factory, who in turn taught the juniors. He would often stand and watch the women working to ensure that his high standards were maintained. He created a particular technique that the factory called 'scrumbling', which enhanced the modelling on a shape and was used for animals and other ornaments; essentially, by emphasising the shadows, the finished

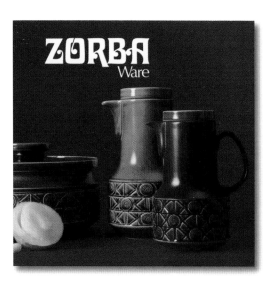

Front cover of a brochure promoting 'Zorba' Ware in the late 1960s.

Publicity
photograph for
'Disneyland'
nurseryware,
1950s.

piece had a depth of colour that distinguished Beswick products from those of its competitors.

Vessels suitable for flower arranging were an important part of the collection. Troughs designed by Hayward and modelled by Mr Symcox in the 1930s remained available to order until the 1960s. These were designed for short-stemmed flowers, and candle holders could be placed in the middle of some of the shapes. As interest in flower arranging as a hobby grew in the 1960s, international experts in floral arrangement were invited to design special shapes. Patricia Easterbrook Roberts created a shallow bowl (shape 1798), which was available both with and without apertures for candlesticks. The design consultant George Smith was commissioned to create a new

Beswick's art
director, Jim
Hayward, at work.

range of containers, and a brochure was published showing how these could be used for both traditional floral arrangements and more modern abstract styles. Colours ranged from white and coloured matt effects to metallic blacks and two-tone mixes such as sage-green and mustard.

Sherry barrel
made in the
early 1960s, and a
dish for Timpsons,
the shoe repairers,
dating from
1964 to 1966.

A wide variety of novelty and advertising wares was also produced. Novelty wares ranged from money-boxes, hen baskets and honey jars to a climbing cat and mouse to fit inside a brandy glass. Many of the quirky and amusing animal sets, such as the cat orchestra, were sold as holiday souvenirs

Two money-boxes in crayon decoration developed by Jim Hayward but modelled by Albert Hallam and issued in the 1960s.

in seaside towns. Advertising wares were a significant aspect of production, and commissions included items for breweries such as Courage, Timpsons shoes, and several whisky and tobacco companies. Many unusual and individual designs were made, for instance Double Diamond teapots and wall plaques and the Dulux dog.

Advertising of Beswick ranges was consistent throughout the early twentieth century but in the mid- to late 1960s new strap-lines were written, including 'It takes a connoisseur to recognise another connoisseur … and it took Beswick to create this brilliant range' and 'A Fine Range of Fancies from Beswick … something to Crow about'. In early 1967 Beswick announced in the *PGGTR* its biggest ever national advertising campaign, using the headline 'You Don't Have to be Gifted to get Beswick horses … Be clever, buy them for yourself'. Colour advertisements were placed in magazines such as *Ideal Home, Horse and Hound, Good Housekeeping* and *Country Life*. Despite the advancing ages of Ewart and Gilbert, Beswick was approaching the end of the decade with every sign of confidence.

'Double Diamond Man', modelled by Hallam and Hayward. This cost 2s 8d to make and was produced between 1958 and 1965.

A NEW OWNER

IN MAY 1962 the *PGGTR* reviewed the state of the pottery industry, tracing its transformation since the war with amalgamations, changes of location, closures, new ventures, 'and a considerable interchange of senior management'. Most businesses were small, employing between one hundred and five hundred workers; only a few firms had more than a thousand employees. Some established family names survived – including Beswick, Doulton, Minton and Aynsley, and in a few companies members of the founding family continued as directors, although often constitutions had changed from private to publicly limited companies, reflecting investment needs after the war, and to avoid death duties for shareholders. Five companies had celebrated centenaries since 1945, and three, bicentenaries; these were achievements that other industries could not easily emulate.

A number of mergers had taken place across the industry: the Lawley group, renamed Allied English Potteries (AEP) in 1964, had acquired thirteen factories including Royal Albert and Royal Crown Derby. Studio pottery was growing, with makers such as Rye Pottery and Honiton Art Pottery thriving. Newcomers to the industry included Hornsea Pottery and Studio Szeiler. Concluding the review are the words 'Historians will call the post-war period by a name such as the pre-Common Market period. It has certainly witnessed great technical and administrative changes, greater perhaps than in any previous period of history.'

Beswick survived this post-war turmoil unscathed, but mergers continued throughout the 1960s. By 1966, 56 per cent of domestic sales came from ten company groups and it was forecast that by 1970 this would reduce to five. In 1968 Royal Doulton and Minton merged, as did J. & G. Meakin with Midwinter, while Wedgwood acquired Johnson Brothers. As costs rose, and credit was squeezed with government restrictions on dividends, it became harder for smaller firms to raise finance for new plant and equipment. Ewart and Gilbert Beswick had no successors and in June 1969 their acceptance of an offer from Royal Doulton of £495,000 made front page news in the *Evening Sentinel*. Together they had guided Beswick

Opposite:
'The Lady Pig' by Amanda Hughes-Lubeck and 'Mrs Rabbit Baking' by Martyn Alcock from the English Country Folk Collection, 1994–9.

47

Dickens wares as jugs, teapots and cruets were very popular from 1934 to 1972, when shapes still being made were discontinued in favour of Royal Doulton ranges. The 'Tony Weller' sugar (far right) was made from 1939 to 1967. Preserve pots were made as part of the teaware series but the middle example would complement many different designs and was produced in lime-green, red or yellow, as well as orange; two versions were made covering the period 1933 to 1970. The preserve pot on the left is part of the 'Springtime' series with a crocus on the lid, 1961–6.

through a turbulent period and their success lies in their understanding of the unique nature of the Beswick name. As a brand Beswick never aspired to be *avant garde*; each generation of Beswicks carefully analysed what other potters were making and strove to produce similar designs at a much lower price. Investment in design and modelling to ensure wares were consistently well potted was an important strategy, and quality was always paramount.

Under the new owner business continued much as before, with Ewart as chairman and Gilbert as sales director. One of the reasons Royal Doulton wanted to purchase Beswick was because it produced earthenware. In the early 1960s Royal Doulton had developed a new ceramic body, English Porcelain, which could be fired in the same kilns as bone china, and this enabled production at the Nile Street factory in Burslem to be streamlined

Farm animals: 'Vietnamese Pot-Bellied Pig' by Amanda Hughes-Lubeck (1999–2002), 'Goat' by Gredington (1945–71), and 'Donkey' by Mr Orwell (1955–2002).

This 'Bald Eagle' by Gredington survived successive culls and was continually in production in a gloss finish from 1945 to 1994. It was also part of the Britannia Collection in the late 1980s.

and made more efficient. Although many of Royal Doulton's former earthenware products were switched to English Porcelain satisfactorily, some items, such as character jugs, were considered better when made from earthenware – and these were transferred to Beswick from August 1972. The Beswick talent for making small-scale character figurines such as the Beatrix Potter Collection led to the Bunnykins Collection, which had a Royal Doulton backstamp although many of the pieces were modelled, as well as made, at the Gold Street factory.

In November 1971 another change was announced: Royal Doulton was to merge with AEP. This change involved a large administrative reorganisation for all factories and personnel. Ewart retired in the spring of 1972 but Gilbert continued to work at the factory and was there in January 1973 to greet the newly appointed executive in charge, Phil Guest.

Beswick ranges were regularly reviewed between the end of the war and 1970, and the shape book reveals several deletion programmes: some are undated but marked with a large cross, while others are dated and were overseen by Ewart between 1967 and 1971. Guest instigated another product rationalisation and, where Ewart had made products obsolete but kept the block and cases,

'Lying Foal', modelled by Arthur Gredington. The brown gloss colourway was in production from 1941 until 2002; between 1989 and 1999 it had a Royal Doulton backstamp.

'Tang Horse', one of two versions made from 1967 to 1972, and now hard to find.

as for Salad and Cottage wares, Guest authorised that these now be destroyed. But the amount of product variety at Beswick was inhibiting the factory's ability to manufacture efficiently and satisfy customer demand, so more changes were needed. Some decisions, Guest recalled, were difficult because Gilbert did not want to end production of any product line – for example, the George Smith flower-arranging containers, or the Fireside penguins, which were made primarily and almost exclusively for an account in the Falkland Islands. Tableware and ornamental shapes were priorities for retirement because these product categories were no longer to be part of the Beswick range.

The Cathay giftware collection modelled by Graham Tongue and launched in 1972 was withdrawn by spring 1973 and pieces are consequently hard to find. Among other shapes made for less than four years between the late 1960s and 1972 are a miniature turkey, a pair of Tang horses, a plaque for Hunts advertising tonic, ginger ale and bitter lemon, a cat cruet set, and a Staffordshire lion and unicorn.

The biggest shock to the Beswick factory was the ending of tableware production – a part of the range since the earliest days of the company. Production capacity was under pressure: orders for horses stretched to

Kitty MacBride's 'Happy Mice' series: 'Just Good Friends', 'A Family Mouse', 'A Snack' and 'Lazybones', modelled by Graham Tongue and David Lyttleton from MacBride's originals, 1975–83.

Rupert Bear

Thelwell

'Rupert Bear' Collection and 'Thelwell' characters, both designed by Sales, produced in the 1980s. The Rupert characters were modelled by Tongue, and Thelwell by Lyttleton.

fifteen weeks, and for Beatrix Potter characters to twenty weeks. 'Zorba' tableware occupied too much factory space, was required in two colours, and orders were poor.

By 1975 much had changed at Beswick; Gilbert had retired, as had Albert Hallam, and Jim Hayward had moved to the Paladin factory – also part of the expanded Royal Doulton group. Harry Sales was design manager and his expertise lay in developing new products for the brand, in which he was ably assisted by Graham Tongue. Younger modellers David Lyttleton (1973–86) and Alan Maslankowski (1973–6) joined the studio, and with Tongue they modelled many of Harry Sales's designs,
including new character ranges such as 'Alice in Wonderland', Kitty MacBride's 'Happy Mice', 'Rupert Bear' and Thelwell ponies, as well as the relief-modelled series of plaques and mugs depicting Christmas scenes from around the world.

Brochure promoting 'Winnie the Pooh', Thelwell, and Rupert Bear, character ranges issued between 1968 and 1989.

Graham Tongue's brilliance as a modeller was only just being appreciated; during the 1960s he had made several bird sculptures but it was not until 1972 that he completed his first horse, a Mountie stallion. Racehorses, including Red Rum, Grundy and Minstrel, were all his work and for each he visited the animal at its stable, where he talked to the horse's trainer and others

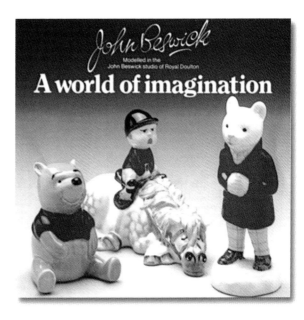

One of a series of studies commissioned by Bass Charrington in the mid-1970s, modelled by Tongue.

Worthington E

'The Spirit of Whitfield' being presented to Princess Anne by Ron Southern, chairman of the Chatterley Whitfield Mining Trust. In 1987 three other models were made: one was auctioned for the Princess's nominated charity, one was given to Chatterley Whitfield, and one to the Beswick museum.

involved with the horse's care, but his main objective was to study the horse – but only when it had relaxed, and this could take half an hour or more. It was at this point that Tongue would assess its character and decide how to convey it in the finished sculpture through pose and expression. Photographs were taken so that details such as markings could be checked when back in the studio.

There Tongue would gradually build up his clay horse model, beginning with proportions taken from bone measurements and then adding structure and texture such as the rib cage, sinews, veins, hair, mane and tail. Horses conform to a precise anatomical form, but the details that he observed and then interpreted in his model are always what captured the horse's unique identity. 'The Spirit of Whitfield', commissioned by the Chatterley Whitfield Mining Museum in 1987, and depicting Kruger, the mine's last pit pony, is Tongue's rarest horse. One of his most dramatic studies, issued in 1994, was Downland Cancara – the stallion famous for advertising Lloyds Bank – which he depicted in its magnificent rearing stance. Tongue also modelled cattle, dogs, fish and wild animals.

Harry Sales left in 1986 and Graham Tongue became design manager, responsible for preliminary drawings for new design ideas as well as continuing with his modelling. He also nurtured the skills of four young sculptors, Warren Platt, Martyn Alcock, Amanda Hughes-Lubeck and Shane Ridge, showing them how to turn their artistic ideas into models that met the requirements of a commercial pottery.

Models of horses and dogs gradually changed, from a show pose to one that showed the animal in action or movement. The white unglazed body of the Spirit Collection was also designed to show up muscle tone and give a more sculptural appearance.

During the 1980s interest in collecting Beswick developed and the first enthusiast to contact Royal Doulton to try to discover more about the brand was Harvey May. The Beswick Collectors Circle, formed in 1985, and renamed the Beswick Collectors Club in 1995, was independent of the company, yet brought together an eager band of

'Standing Cheetah' by Tongue, 1986–95. It was also issued standing on a rock as part of the Connoisseur Collection.

collectors. The Circle supported and cultivated the growing interest in the brand, and the work of enthusiasts such as John and Diana Callow and Marilyn Sweet ensured knowledge was made available to all. The result of this activity was a museum at Gold Street, displaying examples of wares made from the earliest days of the pottery. Pieces were discovered in all corners of the factory and several collectors generously loaned items. The museum opened in 1986 and the first book on Beswick was published in the same year. In 1990 the first Circle exclusive was commissioned – one of a series of collectors' pieces made during the 1990s which are now among the most sought-after of twentieth-century Beswick pieces.

'Setter' from the Spirited Dogs Collection, modelled by Tongue and available in several colourways from 1987 to 1989. A bronze finish, part of the Britannia Collection, was made from 1989 to 1993.

During the mid-1980s and early 1990s a small selection of animals and character studies including Beatrix Potter and Thelwell pieces were made from a resin body. These were not popular and production quickly ended.

Part of the former Beswick museum in 1987. The museum closed in 2002 and many of the pieces were sold at auction at Bonhams, London and Louis Taylor, Hanley in 2003.

From 1989 some Beswick products were rebranded in an effort to gain greater international sales. Beatrix Potter characters were issued with a Royal Albert backstamp until 1998, when they reverted to the Beswick brand. Within this period, studies issued to celebrate anniversaries, such as the centenary of *The Tale of Peter Rabbit*, had Beswick backstamps. Additionally many animals and birds were transferred to a Royal Doulton backstamp. In 1999 animal models remaining in production, together with any new designs, were moved back to a Beswick mark. Between 2000 and 2002 came some fresh studies, including horses produced in association with the Rare Breeds Survival Trust. Modelled by Robert Donaldson, these included an Eriskay pony and a Cleveland Bay. Donaldson also modelled subjects for a collection of rare-breed farm animals comprising sheep and pigs. Character ranges continued to be made in the 1990s with a Beswick backstamp; some, such as 'English Country Folk', 'Cats' Chorus' and 'Pig Promenade' are comparatively easy to find but others, such as 'The Herbs' and 'Trumpton', are scarcer as they were made only in 2001.

But the days of the Beswick brand at the Gold Street Works were numbered. The ceramic industry was under severe pressure and Royal Doulton had no choice but to make sweeping cuts. At the end of 2002 production of Beswick ended and in 2003 the Gold Street site, which had been used for pottery production since at least 1846, was sold to property developers. It is now a retail park, but this was not the end of the Beswick story.

'Cats' Chorus', modelled by Shane Ridge and produced from 1998 to 2001. Two more characters, 'Fat Cat' and 'Glam Guitar', added in 1999, completed the collection.

'I love you as high as I can reach'

THE TWENTY-FIRST CENTURY

THE CERAMIC INDUSTRY in the early twenty-first century operates in a vastly different way compared to the mid-twentieth century, let alone fifty years before that. Manufacturers have to compete not just with a factory 5 miles away but with ones on the other side of the world. For many brands to survive, products have to be manufactured in other countries where costs are lower, so that products are available at prices that consumers will pay. As factories have disappeared in the Potteries, so have many famous brand names, but the strength of the Beswick brand, and in particular its identification with animal sculpture, have ensured that it is one of the few names that have survived.

In 2005 a Yorkshire entrepreneur, John Sinclair, bought the Beswick brand, including production moulds and archive material, from Royal Doulton. The son of a china retailer and a retailer himself, he remembers the affection that customers had for Beswick in the 1950s and 1960s, when figurines were bought as gifts for children and adults who loved animals and wanted a small, well-made memento to mark their passion. By buying the brand, he wanted to save it from extinction. Two collections were launched, Beswick England – a prestigious range including limited editions made in Stoke-on-Trent – and John Beswick, an inexpensive range featuring animals and character studies manufactured overseas.

It was also important to John Sinclair and to John Hammond, who joined him as a director of the company, that the new sculptures should emulate the qualities of Beswick animals made in the post-war period, such as their feel, weight, styles of coloration and decoration – qualities that had been lost in the late twentieth century. With the ceramic designer and sculptor Richard Wawrzesta they have experimented with glazes and ceramic colours to achieve the best effects, while incorporating many recent technological developments.

To avoid any confusion between old and new Beswick, fresh sculptures and production moulds were and are commissioned for both ranges and all of the Beswick England collection is marked with the year of manufacture. There are three exceptions, however, since when Sinclair looked at the

Opposite:
Hare, from the
'Guess How
Much I Love You'
Collection by
Anita Jeram;
John Beswick
backstamp.

Stag, limited edition of one hundred, modelled by Amanda Hughes-Lubeck; Beswick England backstamp.

'Przewalski's horse' by Amanda Hughes-Lubeck; Beswick England backstamp; limited edition of one thousand.

moulds he realised there were some designs that had never been released and these became the first three horses under the Beswick England mark. The first was 'Przewalski's horse', originally modelled by Amanda Hughes-Lubeck in the mid 1990s, followed by 'Camargue' and 'Mustang'. The Beswick England collection has since grown to include 'Huntsman' and 'Huntswoman', a study of the Queen on Burmese, a pair of sheepdogs and a majestic stag.

For both ranges quality is an absolute prerequisite and this starts with the British-based design process. Richard Wawrzesta has modelled most of the studies for the John Beswick Collection and, as well as making the original models, he also produces the moulds and decorates the first pieces, which are used as standards for subsequent production.

The launch collection in 2006 was broad, with over thirty models including birds, dogs, wildlife and horses. Alongside traditional Beswick subjects of Shire horses, Labrador dogs, robins, owls, blue tits and kittens were more unusual subjects such as a woodcock – which had not previously been included in a Beswick range. In the past Beswick was happy to offer animal sculptures in a variety of colourways, and choice has also been included in the modern ranges, with horses and dogs in shades appropriate to each breed.

'Woodcock', modelled by Richard Wawrzesta; John Beswick Collection.

Humorous character animals such as pigs, ducklings and chicks, as well as licensed series, have also become part of the John Beswick range. Notable are the Snowman, Thelwell, Bryn Parry and Anita Jeram collections.

Wawrzesta is upholding the long tradition of Beswick sculptors demonstrating a passion for animals and wildlife, and an innate ability to see and incorporate the comic and curious in life in his work. Creating a character model from a two-dimensional drawing is different from a realistic animal study but the key to both is astute observation, and he uses his appreciation of the curious way animals stand or hold their heads and tails to create the characters that illustrators such as Norman Thelwell have drawn.

'Vanner Pony', piebald colourway, modelled by Richard Wawrzesta; John Beswick Collection.

For animal studies, Wawrzesta works from memory, photographs and real animals. He says:

> On the surface, one cow can look pretty much like another but there are many differences and it is vital to capture these small variations in traits that are important to farmers and the breed experts. Since every expert has a different opinion as to what makes a true champion it is my job to find a happy medium bringing together the best of all beliefs to create the perfect specimen. Cats or more humorous studies such as the duckling and chick families and the trio of pigs do not need the same level of detail, as for these it's more important to capture the spirit or character of the animal and to show them interacting.

'Rabbit', 'Hedgehog' and 'Otter', modelled by Richard Wawrzesta; John Beswick Collection.

'Springer' from the
Bryn Parry series;
John Beswick
backstamp.

'Father Christmas'
from the book of
the same name by
Raymond Briggs;
John Beswick
backstamp.

In a sense the aims and ideals of the Beswick
brand are the same in the twenty-first century
as at the beginning of the twentieth.
Production and ranges are flexible to take into
account the changing demands of customers
and collectors. And the philosophy behind the
company has long been a familiar one: to produce
well-designed and well-modelled animal
sculptures and other wares at an affordable
price. The ceramic industry has changed
beyond all recognition over the twentieth
century but remarkably the Beswick name
has survived and it can only be hoped that
its products will continue to give pleasure
for another generation to come.

FURTHER INFORMATION

FURTHER READING

Callow, D. and J. *A Charlton Standard Catalogue: Beswick Pottery*. Charlton Press, second edition 1999. Includes ornamental and table wares, and a price guide.

Callow, D. and J, and Corley, F. *A Charlton Standard Catalogue: Beswick Collectables*. Charlton Press, tenth edition 2009. Includes Beatrix Potter, character jugs, figurines and other models inspired by television, film and literature, and a price guide.

Callow, D. and J., and Sweet, M. and P. *A Charlton Standard Catalogue: Beswick Animals*. Charlton Press, tenth edition 2011. Includes animals and price guide.

May, H. *The Beswick Price Guide*. Francis Joseph, fourth edition 1997.

May, H., Baynton, V., and Morton, J. *The Beswick Collector's Handbook*. Kevin Francis Publishing Limited, 1986. The first publication about Beswick includes details on modellers and designers.

Pinhas, O. *Goldscheider*. Richard Dennis, 2006.

Pottery Gazette and Glass Trade Review. Copies held at Stoke-on-Trent City Archives, City Central Library, Bethesda Street, Hanley, Stoke-on-Trent ST1 3RS. Telephone: 01782 238420.

Warburton, W. H. *History of Trade Union Organisation in North Staffordshire Potteries*. Allen & Unwin, London, 1931. For discussion of disputes, wages and changes in conditions in the early twentieth century.

MAGAZINES

Beswick Collectors Club: www.beswickcollectorsclub.com

Collecting Doulton and Beswick Magazine: www.collectingdoulton.com

WEBSITE

John Beswick Ltd: www.johnbeswick.co.uk

PLACES TO VISIT

Gladstone Pottery Museum, Uttoxeter Road, Longton, Stoke-on-Trent ST3 1PQ. Telephone: 01782 237777. Website: www.stokemuseums.org.uk Experience life in a Victorian pottery.

Hill Top, Near Sawrey, Hawkshead, Ambleside, Cumbria LA22 0LF. Telephone: 015394 36269. One of many places in Cumbria linked to Beatrix Potter. Discover more at www.visitcumbria.com

Potteries Museum and Art Gallery, Cultural Quarter, Stoke-on-Trent ST1 3DW. Telephone: 01782 232323. Website: www.stoke.gov.uk Extensive collection of twentieth-century ceramics.

Opposite page: 'Cancara', modelled by Tongue and based on Downland Cancara, famous for advertising Lloyds Bank. It is shown with its swing ticket promoting 100 years of Beswick, 1894–94.

INDEX

Page numbers in italics refer to illustrations